W9-ALV-734

Ripley's—
Believe It or Not! ®

ODD PLACES

A Byron Preiss Book

TOR

A TOM DOHERTY ASSOCIATES BOOK
NEW YORK
RL 4.8 IL 011-013

The Ripley's 100th Anniversary Series:

Weird Inventions and Discoveries
Odd Places
Strange Coincidences
Wild Animals
Reptiles, Lizards and Prehistoric Beasts
Great and Strange Works of Man

Ripley's Believe It or Not!
Odd Places

Copyright © 1991 by Ripley Entertainment, Inc.

Cover design by Dean Motter
Interior design by William Mohalley
Edited by Howard Zimmerman

A TOR Book
Published by Tom Doherty Associates, Inc.
175 Fifth Ave.
New York, New York 10010

ISBN: 0-812-51285-5

First Tor edition: May 1991

Printed in the United States of America

0 9 8 7 6 5 4 3 2

INTRODUCTION

Welcome to the special Centennial Edition of "Ripley's Believe It or Not!", the most famous and best known entertainment feature in the world. The centennial series is designed to help celebrate the forthcoming hundredth anniversary of Robert L. Ripley's birth in 1993.

Ripley was one of the most fabulous and interesting personalities of the 20th century. He spent his life traveling the globe in pursuit of the odd, bizarre, and incredible-but-true stories that have filled the "Believe It or Not!" pages for over 70 years. During this period, more than 80 million people in 125 countries have been entertained and amazed by Robert L. Ripley's creation. In addition, millions more have marveled at the incredible oddities on display at the Ripley's museums in America, England, Canada, Australia, and Japan.

Ripley's amazing worldwide industry is a true American success story, for it started humbly with one man and an idea.

In 1918, the twenty-five-year-old Ripley was a hard-working sports cartoonist for the New York Globe newspaper. It happened one day that he was stuck for a cartoon to draw. As his daily deadline approached, he was still staring at a blank sheet on

T 1985

his drawing board when inspiration struck. Ripley dug into his files where he kept notes on all sorts of unusual sports achievements. He quickly sketched nine of the more interesting and bizarre items onto his page, and a legend was born. That first page was titled "Champs and Chumps." Ripley's editor quickly came up with a snappier name, and "Believe It or Not!" became an overnight sensation.

In 1929, Ripley published his very first collection of "Believe It or Not!" in book form. It was an immediate success. A few years later his feature was appearing in over 200 newspapers in the United States and Canada alone. But Ripley was just getting started. With financial backing from his newspaper syndicate, Ripley traveled thousands of miles in the next few years. He visited 198 countries, bringing back oddities, antiques, and amazing stories from each place he stopped. The best of these eventually wound up in his famous syndicated feature. The amazing truth is that Ripley supplied at least one "Believe It or Not!" every day for thirty years!

In 1933, Ripley collected many of his fabulous treasures and put them on exhibition in Chicago. Within a year, his "Odditorium" had hosted almost two and a half million people. They lined up around the block to see the displays of shrunken heads, postage-stamp-size paintings, treasures from the Orient, incredibly intricate matchstick models, and wickedly gleaming instruments of medieval torture.

Soon after Ripley died in 1949, his unique collection of oddities was gathered and displayed in the first permanent "Believe It or Not!" museum in St. Augustine, Florida. And, fittingly, Ripley himself became one of its more amazing items. A full-size replica of the man stood at the door, greeting all visitors and giving them a foretaste of the astonishing objects they would see inside.

Although Robert L. Ripley passed away, his work lives on. The Ripley's organization has ceaselessly provided daily "Believe It or Not!" pages through the decades, always reaching a bit farther for those fantastic (but true) stories that stretch the imagination. And they are still actively seeking more. If you know of any amazing oddity, write it down and send it in to:

Ripley's Believe It or Not!
90 Eglinton Avenue East, Suite 510
Toronto, Canada
M4P 2Y3

There are now over 110,000 "Believe It or Not!" cartoons that have been printed in over 300 categories. These include everything from amazing animals to catastrophes to "Odd Places," the volume you hold right now. So sit back, get comfortable, and prepare to be astonished, surprised, amazed and delighted. Believe it or not!

THE **COUNTY COURTHOUSE** IN LABRADOR FOR MANY YEARS WAS LOCATED ON A YACHT-- WHICH EACH SUMMER CRUISED THE COAST AND ADMINISTERED JUSTICE

THE **RAINIEST SPOT
IN THE WORLD
MT. WAIALEALE**
Hawaii,
HAS AN AVERAGE
ANNUAL RAINFALL OF
460 INCHES A YEAR

THE SHIP THAT BECAME AN ISLAND
A SAILING SHIP ABANDONED IN THE MARONI RIVER BETWEEN
FRENCH AND DUTCH GUIANA, FILLED WITH SOIL AND SPROUTED
TREES AND PLANTS--*ALL IN A PERIOD OF 36 YEARS*

THE **GREAT SPHINX** at Giza, in Egypt IS 66 FT. HIGH AND 240 FT. LONG YET IT HAS ALMOST BEEN COVERED BY SAND MANY TIMES

A EUROPEAN BORDER THAT IS CROSSED WITHOUT A PASSPORT!

Travelers can cross the border between Germany and Austria in a salt mine at Hallein, Austria, traversing a series of slides at up to 40 mph —*SITTING ASTRIDE A HARDWOOD RAIL*

THE WORLD'S NARROWEST DRAWBRIDGE
THE SOMERSET BRIDGE IN BERMUDA HAS AN 18-INCH-WIDE WOODEN FLAP TO ALLOW THE MASTS OF *SAILBOATS* TO GO THROUGH

THE NUT MUSEUM FOUNDED
BY ELIZABETH TASHJIAN IN
OLD LYME, CONN., EXHIBITS
NUTS OF EVERY KIND FROM
ALL OVER THE WORLD INCLUDING
A 35 LB. DOUBLE COCONUT

The **HOT SPRINGS**
of Beppu, Japan,
USED BY THE JAPANESE FOR
HEALTH BATHING, PRODUCE
MORE THAN 10,000,000
GALLONS OF SCALDING
WATER EVERY 24 HOURS

The **WHISPERING GALLERY**
in the Dome of Gol-Gumaz, in Bijapur, India,
ECHOES THE SOUND OF LAUGHTER 20 TIMES --
YET ALL OTHER SOUNDS ARE ECHOED
ONLY 10 TIMES

A STATUE OF AN OIL DRILLER in Tulsa, Okla., STANDS 76 FEET HIGH, WEIGHS 45,000 POUNDS AND WEARS A SIZE 112 HARD HAT

A MONUMENT TO A LIAR

A FOUNTAIN IN BODENWERDER, W. GERMANY, DEPICTS BARON KARL Von MUNCHAUSEN RIDING HALF A HORSE--A MEMORIAL TO HIS TALL TALE THAT DURING THE TURKISH WARS HE RODE HALF A HORSE TO VICTORY ...

THE **ALFALFA PALACE** in Fallon, Nevada, BUILT IN 1915 TO HOUSE THE AGRICULTURAL EXHIBIT AT THE STATE FAIR, WAS CONSTRUCTED ENTIRELY FROM *54 TONS OF HAY*

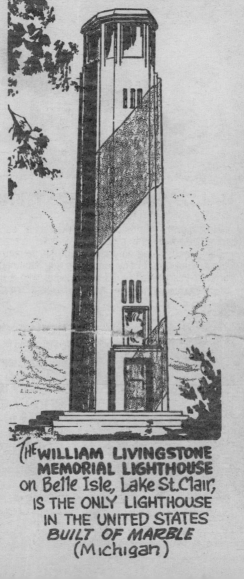

THE **WILLIAM LIVINGSTONE MEMORIAL LIGHTHOUSE** on Belle Isle, Lake St. Clair, IS THE ONLY LIGHTHOUSE IN THE UNITED STATES *BUILT OF MARBLE* (Michigan)

BALDASARE FORESTIERE
(1879-1946)
an Italian immigrant who had once worked as a ''sandhog''
building New York City's subways, moved to Fresno,
Calif., and, using only a pick and shovel and
without blueprints of any kind, dug singlehandedly,
over a 37-year period, a 35-room home, with a mile
of connecting tunnels— *ALL UNDERGROUND*

A HOUSE OF A DIFFERENT COLOR!
ONE SIDE OF AN
APARTMENT HOUSE
OWNED BY MARK VAN
NOPPEN AND TYLER
ROBERTS IN PROVI-
DENCE, R.I., WAS
GIVEN AN
ELABORATE COLOR-
BY-NUMBERS LOOK--
*INCLUDING CRAYON
SCRAWLS AND THREE
17-FOOT CRAYONS!*

A DINER

once opened by band leader
Lawrence Welk in
Mason City,
Ia., was shaped like an
accordion and featured on
its menu
"SQUEEZEBURGERS"

THE **RAILROAD STATION** IN SAVONA, ITALY, CONSTRUCTED IN 1962, *HAS NO RAILROAD*

THE DEXTER SALOON
IN PANAMINT CITY, CA., IN THE 1800's HAD SO MANY GUNFIGHTS THAT ITS WALLS *WERE COVERED WITH BULLET-PROOF METAL*

THE CHURCH THAT WAS FOUND BY A DREAM

THE CHURCH OF STAVROS NOW USED FOR REGULAR SERVICES ON THE ISLAND OF PERISSA, GREECE, HAD BEEN BURIED FOR 400 YEARS UNTIL A FARMER NAMED GERASSIMOS, IN THE VILLAGE OF GONIA, GREECE, SAW THE LOCATION OF THE LOST EDIFICE *IN A DREAM!*

A **RESTAURANT**
IN A SUBURB OF LOS ANGELES, CA., IN THE 1930S WAS SHAPED *LIKE A BULLDOG*

"POLYNYA"

A lake discovered by a joint team of American and Russian explorers in the heart of the Antarctic ice pack, appears and disappears and sometimes covers an area of 100,000 sq. miles — but it is completely *FREE OF ICE*

ONE-MAN CHURCH

THE MADONNA CHAPEL -of Bayou Goula, La.,

IS JUST LARGE ENOUGH TO ACCOMMODATE THE PRIEST
WHILE SAYING MASS

The Worshipers Must Remain Outside

FRANCIS and MURRIL DAELLENBACH
FOR 14 YEARS HAVE LIVED 17 FEET UNDERGROUND NEAR CHUGWATER, WY., IN A *FORMER MISSILE SILO*

THE NORTH MAGNETIC POLE AT WHICH COMPASSES POINT, HAS MOVED 480 MILES TO THE NORTHWEST SINCE 1904 -- WHICH IS 800 MILES SOUTH OF THE REAL NORTH POLE

THE **LIGHTHOUSE**
AT CAPE HATTERAS,
NEAR BUXTON, N·C·,
208 FEET HIGH,
*IS THE TALLEST
LIGHTHOUSE IN THE U.S.*

HOUSE BUILT ENTIRELY OF TOMBSTONES
Owned by O. E. YOUNG, Petersburg, Va.

THE SINGULAR YANCEY HOUSE
IN Forest Park, Ga

RAIN FALLING ON THE FRONT VERANDA
FLOWS INTO THE GULF OF MEXICO —
RAIN FALLING ON THE BACK VERANDA
FLOWS INTO THE ATLANTIC OCEAN

JOSEFSBERG

a village in South Tyrol, Italy,

IS IN PERPETUAL SHADOW
FOR 91 DAYS EACH YEAR

*MOUNTAINS CUT OFF THE SUN
FROM NOV. 3 UNTIL FEB. 2*

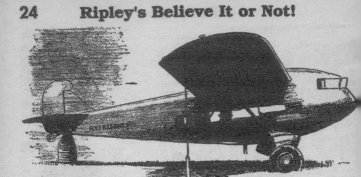

A **$320,000** <u>HOT DOG STAND</u>!

A TWIN-MOTORED CABIN PLANE
— AN EXPERIMENT COSTING
ITS BACKERS $320,000 <u>00</u>
MADE BUT **ONE** FLIGHT AND WAS
LATER TURNED INTO A HOT DOG
STAND AT THE FORD AIRPORT
Lansing, Ill

THE PALACE OF THE MARSH ARABS

in Arabia has huge archways made of
BUNDLES OF RUSHES!

THE AMAZING
WATERFALL OF KAPILATIRTHAM
India
ITS FLOW ALWAYS INCREASES
DURING PERIODS OF DROUGHT!

THE **BAT** TEMPLE NEAR KLUNGKUNG, BALI, LOCATED INSIDE A MOUNTAIN CAVE, *SHELTERS HUNDREDS OF THOUSANDS OF BATS*

THE **CONE HOMES** OF **CAPPADOCIA** TURKEY, **ROCK CONES CREATED BY A NOW EXTINCT VOLCANO,** AND OCCUPIED BY TURKISH FARMERS, *WERE HOLLOWED OUT AS CELLS AND CHAPELS BY EARLY CHRISTIANS AND HAVE AS MANY AS 10 FLOORS*

THE FIRST MOTION PICTURE STUDIO

CREATED BY THOMAS ALVA EDISON IN EAST ORANGE, N.J., IN 1893, WAS MOUNTED ON A PIVOT SO ITS STAGE COULD BE TURNED TO THE SUN-- *AND COST $637*

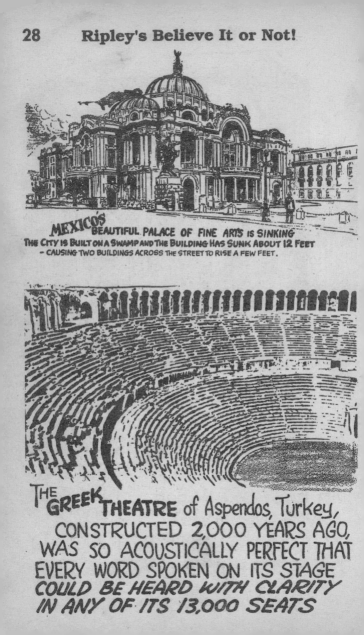

MEXICO'S BEAUTIFUL PALACE OF FINE ARTS IS SINKING
THE CITY IS BUILT ON A SWAMP AND THE BUILDING HAS SUNK ABOUT 12 FEET
– CAUSING TWO BUILDINGS ACROSS THE STREET TO RISE A FEW FEET.

THE **GREEK THEATRE** of Aspendos, Turkey, CONSTRUCTED 2,000 YEARS AGO, WAS SO ACOUSTICALLY PERFECT THAT EVERY WORD SPOKEN ON ITS STAGE *COULD BE HEARD WITH CLARITY IN ANY OF ITS 13,000 SEATS*

THE **POLICE STATION**
OF CARRABELLE, FLA., IS AN
OUTDOOR TELEPHONE BOOTH

ATRANI
A VILLAGE OF 2,600 IN ITALY, CONSISTING OF HOUSES JAMMED TOGETHER BETWEEN A ROCKY MOUNTAIN AND THE SEA, *DOES NOT HAVE A SINGLE STREET TRAVERSING IT*

CASTILLO DE SAN MARCOS
A STAR-SHAPED FORT, BUILT BETWEEN 1672 AND 1695, AT THE EDGE OF MATANZAS BAY IN ST. AUGUSTINE, FLA., IS CONSTRUCTED PARTIALLY OF SEA SHELLS --- YET, DESPITE MANY ATTACKS ON IT, THE FORT HAS NEVER BEEN TAKEN!

SLOVENSKA NARODNA PODPORNA JEDNOTA

a town in Pennsylvania has one of the longest names in the U.S. — but it has only 11 residents, one mail box, one pay phone and covers only 500 acres.

A HOME
IN ARZACHENA, SARDINIA, THAT WAS
HOLLOWED OUT OF A GIANT BOULDER-
A DOOR WAS BUILT INTO THE BOULDER
AND ITS OUTER WALL IS COVERED WITH
SMALL STONES AS A DECORATIVE GESTURE

THE SKYDOME STADIUM IN
TORONTO, CANADA, IS BIG
ENOUGH TO HOLD OVER
1,200 *ELEPHANTS AND
EIGHT 747 AIRPLANES!*

THE CASTLE OF THE CAVE
IN SLOVENIA, YUGOSLAVIA,
A FORTRESS CONSTRUCTED BY THE
KOBENZL FAMILY IN 1570, IS LOCATED
*IN A LARGE CAVE AT THE FOOT
OF A 426-FOOT CLIFF.*
IT IS NOW A WORLD WAR II MUSEUM

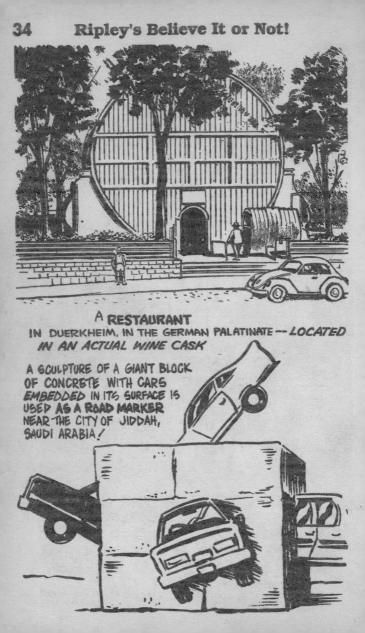

A **RESTAURANT** IN DUERKHEIM, IN THE GERMAN PALATINATE -- *LOCATED IN AN ACTUAL WINE CASK*

A SCULPTURE OF A GIANT BLOCK OF CONCRETE WITH CARS EMBEDDED IN ITS SURFACE IS USED AS A ROAD MARKER NEAR THE CITY OF JIDDAH, SAUDI ARABIA!

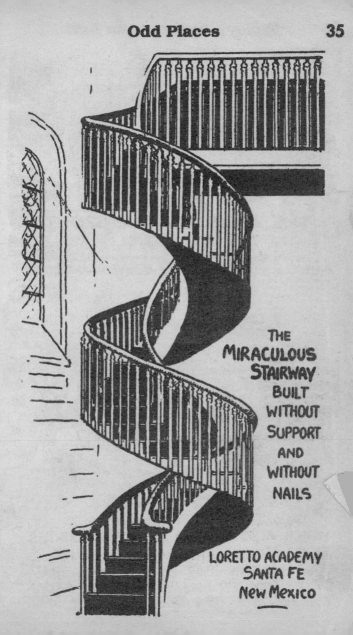

THE
MIRACULOUS
STAIRWAY
BUILT
WITHOUT
SUPPORT
AND
WITHOUT
NAILS

LORETTO ACADEMY
SANTA FE
New Mexico

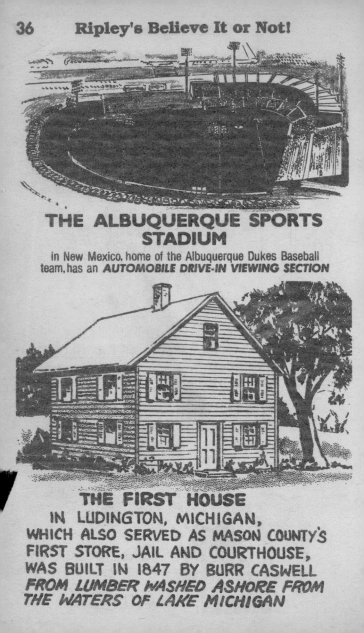

THE ALBUQUERQUE SPORTS STADIUM

in New Mexico, home of the Albuquerque Dukes Baseball team, has an *AUTOMOBILE DRIVE-IN VIEWING SECTION*

THE FIRST HOUSE

IN LUDINGTON, MICHIGAN, WHICH ALSO SERVED AS MASON COUNTY'S FIRST STORE, JAIL AND COURTHOUSE, WAS BUILT IN 1847 BY BURR CASWELL *FROM LUMBER WASHED ASHORE FROM THE WATERS OF LAKE MICHIGAN*

THE **HOME**
OF ALFRED REXROTH IN
LOHR, GERMANY, IS BUILT
AROUND A 241-FT. FIR
TREE THAT EXTENDS
THROUGH ITS ROOF

PETE FALCIONE

operates a 50-tank ''fish hotel'' in Norwalk, Conn., for
boarding fish. They are kept in aquariums that match
the chemical balance of their home tanks — and fed on
either the one-meal-a-day European plan or an American
plan, providing *CUSTOM, GOURMET DIETS!*

AMERICA'S STONEHENGE

MYSTERY HILL, AN ANCIENT VILLAGE IN NEW HAMPSHIRE,
CONTAINING A HUGE STONE SACRIFICIAL TABLE,
MAY HAVE BEEN FOUNDED IN 2,000 B.C.

HIGH PARKING
A GARAGE IN AN ATTIC!
HOUSE BUILT ON A HILLSIDE—
THE LIVING QUARTERS ARE BELOW THE GARAGE
Sausalito, California

THE CHURCH OF THE HABÉ TRIBE – Sudan
IS COPIED FROM THE GIANT ANT NESTS THAT ABOUND IN THE COUNTRY
ORIGINALLY THE ACTUAL ANT NESTS WERE EMPLOYED FOR THEIR HOUSE OF WORSHIP!

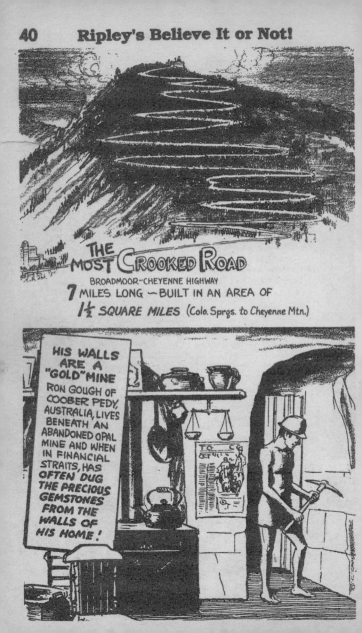

THE MOST CROOKED ROAD

BROADMOOR-CHEYENNE HIGHWAY
7 MILES LONG — BUILT IN AN AREA OF
1½ SQUARE MILES (Colo. Sprgs. to Cheyenne Mtn.)

HIS WALLS ARE A "GOLD" MINE

RON GOUGH OF COOBER PEDY, AUSTRALIA, LIVES BENEATH AN ABANDONED OPAL MINE AND WHEN IN FINANCIAL STRAITS, HAS OFTEN DUG THE PRECIOUS GEMSTONES FROM THE WALLS OF HIS HOME!

A **COUNTRY STORE**
ON THE SORLAND COAST OF NORWAY,
LOCATED ON AN OTHERWISE
UNINHABITED ROCKY ISLAND, CAN
BE REACHED ONLY BY BOAT

TOED INN
A RESTAURANT IN LOS ANGELES, CA., IN THE 1940s--*SHAPED LIKE A HUGE TOAD*

UNDERGROUND CHURCH
CARVED FROM SOLID SALT! — WIELICZKA, Poland
A COMPLETE CITY HAS BEEN BUILT IN THESE SALT MINES WHERE **1500** MEN WORK DAILY.

THE STANDLEY CHASM IN THE MacDonnell Mountains of Australia, **20** FEET WIDE AND **500** FEET DEEP, IS A CLEFT SO DARK THAT A MAN STANDING AT THE BOTTOM OF IT *CAN SEE STARS IN THE DAYTIME*

DRAWN FROM SKETCHES MADE IN THE CHURCH OF SAN NICOLA, BARI, ITALY 1937

TOMB OF SANTA CLAUS

SANTA CLAUS REALLY *LIVED* — HE WAS THE BISHOP OF MYRA — IN ASIA MINOR.
HE DIED DEC. 6, 342 A.D. AND IS *BURIED* IN THE CHURCH OF ST. NICHOLAS BARI,
ITALY. ST. NICHOLAS WAS NOT ONLY THE PATRON SAINT OF CHILDREN—
BUT OF **THIEVES** AND **PAWNBROKERS!**

THE **HOME** of the HANGMAN OF NUREMBERG, GERMANY,
WAS A TOWER IN THE MIDDLE OF THE PEGNITZ RIVER BRIDGE
-- *BECAUSE NO ONE WANTED TO LIVE NEAR A HANGMAN*

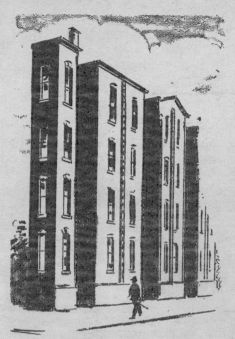

"THE SPITE HOUSE"

A HOME BUILT AT LEXINGTON AVENUE AND 82nd STREET, IN NEW YORK CITY, IN 1882, WAS ONLY 5 FEET WIDE AT EACH END.
IT WAS CONSTRUCTED BY JOSEPH RICHARDSON TO SPITE THE OWNER OF ADJACENT APARTMENT HOUSES, AND WAS OCCUPIED BY HIM UNTIL HIS DEATH 15 YEARS LATER

THE SINGING SANDS OF THE GOBI DESERT
WIND, BLOWING OVER THE SAND DUNES, CAUSES A CONSTANT SOUND THAT VARIES FROM A ROLL OF DRUMS TO A DEEP CHANT

RAINBOW LAKE

A VOLCANIC CRATER LAKE ON THE WEST COAST OF LANZAROTE IN THE CANARY ISLANDS, BECAUSE OF LAYERS OF LAVA CONSTANTLY DISPLAYS **6** *DIFFERENT COLORS*

THE **SUMMER TENTS** USED BY ESKIMOS IN BAFFINLAND IN THE CANADIAN ARCTIC HAVE WALLS MADE OF SEALSKINS, BUT THE FRONT IS ALWAYS MADE OF MEMBRANE STRIPPED FROM THE INSIDE OF THE PELT *TO LET IN THE LIGHT*

THE TRANSIENT CHURCH in Jamestown, R.I.
IT WAS DESIGNED BY THE REV. CHARLES E. PRESTON IN 1899, SO IT COULD BE MOVED FROM PLACE TO PLACE BY 14 YOKE OF OXEN

THE SACRED MEMORIAL
TO MOGUL EMPEROR AKBAR, (1542-1602) LOCATED IN THE FORT OF AGRA, INDIA, *IS THE BATHTUB HE USED FOR 36 YEARS*

KITTY
WITCHES'
ROW
—Gt. Yarmouth, Eng.
IS SO NARROW THAT AT
ONE POINT IT IS ONLY
1 FT. 11½ IN. WIDE!

THE **BATTLE MONUMENT** IN BENNINGTON, VERMONT, COMMEMORATING THE 1777 BATTLE OF BENNINGTON, IS THE TALLEST BATTLE MONUMENT IN THE WORLD—MEASURING *302 FEET*

A HOLLOW TREE IN THE YOSEMITE VALLEY WITH AN AREA 21 FEET BY 16 FEET WAS USED FOR 3 YEARS BY A MOUNTAINEER NAMED A. J. SMITH *AS HIS HOME AND AS A STABLE FOR HIS HORSE*

The
ICE MINE — A FREAK OF NATURE
STRANGE ICE FORMATIONS AND MAMMOTH ICICLES
FORM DURING *HOT* WEATHER – AND THAW OUT
IN COLD WEATHER.
Coudersport, Pa.

THE **NORDERNEY LIGHTHOUSE**, GERMANY, 197 FEET HIGH— TO ENABLE IT TO WITHSTAND THE VIOLENT WINDS WAS BUILT SO THAT IT SWAYS AS MUCH AS *2 FEET OFF CENTER*

A **STATUE** IN BIERVLIET, NETHERLANDS ERECTED TO WILLEM BEUKELSZ --FAMED FOR INVENTING A NEW METHOD OF *GUTTING A HERRING*

THE HIGHEST BRIDGE
IN THE WORLD
1053 FT. ABOVE THE RIVER

Royal Gorge
Colorado

A **CHURCH** BUILT BY CHARLES WALENSKY in Waterloo, Iowa, IS ONLY SIX FEET WIDE, EIGHT FEET LONG *AND SEATS ONLY FOUR PERSONS*

GOOD BUILDINGS COME IN SMALL BOTTLES EDUOAD ARSENAULT OF CAP-EGMONT ON CANADA'S PRINCE EDWARD ISLAND, CONSTRUCTED 3 BUILDINGS OUT OF GLASS BOTTLES. THE FIRST WAS BUILT WITH 12,000, THE SECOND WITH 8,000 AND THE THIRD WAS A CHURCH THAT EVEN HAD "STAINED" GLASS WINDOWS

THE CATHEDRAL of BARCELONA

n Spain, WAS STARTED IN 1249 AND
NOT COMPLETED UNTIL 1913
664 YEARS LATER

MORE DEAD THAN ALIVE!

COLMA, CALIF., WITH 14 CEMETERIES, HAS A DEAD
POPULATION OF OVER 1,000,000 -- WHILE THE
LIVING TOTAL ONLY *750 -- YET THE TOWN
HAS NO FUNERAL HOMES* ··

LUXURIOUS YACHTS

CRUISING THE EPINAL CANAL IN THE NORTH OF FRANCE, CROSS
OVER THE MOSELLE RIVER ON A 100-YEAR-OLD BRIDGE
MORE THAN ONE MILE LONG--WITH WATER 7½ FEET DEEP!

THE GENERAL NOBLE
REDWOOD TREE HOUSE
LONG A LANDMARK IN
WASHINGTON, D.C., WAS BUILT
FROM THE STUMP OF A GIANT
CALIFORNIA SEQUOIA THAT
*TOOK LUMBERJACKS A
WEEK TO CUT THROUGH*

MONUMENT TO A COW

THIS MONUMENT, ERECTED
BY THE BUTCHERS OF
TOKYO IN 1931, MARKS
THE SPOT ON WHICH THE
FIRST COW IN JAPAN WAS
SLAUGHTERED IN 1858
FOR HUMAN CONSUMPTION
Temple Yard, Shimoda

THE GOVERNMENT HOUSE
IN AUCKLAND, N.Z., WAS BUILT IN ENGLAND IN 1840,
THEN DISMANTLED AND SHIPPED BY BOAT TO NEW ZEALAND WHERE
IT SERVED AS A RESIDENCE OF THE GOVERNOR FOR 8 YEARS

THE
BRIDGE
THAT MAKES THE DEVIL DIZZY
SHANGHAI
CONSTRUCTED TO MISLEAD THE DEVIL
BY ITS ANGLES AND ZIG-ZAGS

THE AMAZING FLOATING GARDENS OF LAKE TAL

FARMERS in Kashmir **CUT STRIPS OF MARSHLAND 20 YARDS LONG, 3 FEET WIDE AND 2 FEET THICK AND ANCHOR THEM IN LAKE TAL WITH POLES TO SERVE AS** *FLOATING GARDENS* **ROTTING WEEDS DREDGED UP FROM THE LAKE BOTTOM ARE ADDED FROM TIME TO TIME TO ENRICH THE SOIL**

A RESTAURANT IN NICE, FRANCE, SERVES A GOURMET MEAL FOR DOGS, INCLUDING APERITIF, MAIN COURSE AND DESSERT FOR $9

THE 5 CHAPELS
of the Capucine Church, in Rome, Italy,
ARE LINED WITH HUMAN SKELETONS AND BONES
-SOME OF THE SKELETONS ATTIRED AS MONKS

THE **HOTEL WIEN**
IN KOTZEBUE, ALASKA,
ON THE ARCTIC OCEAN,
IS THE NORTHERNMOST HOTEL IN THE WORLD

THE **TOMB**
of the 13th Dalai Lama of Tibet, in Lhasa,
IS COVERED WITH 300,000 OUNCES OF SOLID
GOLD – *VALUED AT $10,500,000*

THE **STATUE** of EMPEROR MARCUS AURELIUS IN ROME, ITALY, WAS USED IN THE MIDDLE AGES AS A GALLOWS-- CRIMINALS WERE HANGED BY A ROPE LOOPED AROUND THE HORSE'S HEAD

AQUAPOLIS
A FLOATING COMMUNITY
OFF OKINAWA, JAPAN,
OFFERS HOUSING AT A
LOWER RENTAL THAN
TYPICAL TOKYO
APARTMENTS

REAL de CATORCE
A FORMER MINING TOWN IN MEXICO,
IS THE ONLY COMMUNITY IN THE
WESTERN HEMISPHERE THAT CAN BE
ENTERED ONLY BY A TUNNEL

THE TALLEST STAIRWAY

IN THE WORLD – Djebel Musa, Sinai

2100 FEET HIGH – 3000 STEPS – LEADING TO
THE TOP OF THE MOUNTAIN WHERE MOSES
RECEIVED THE TABLETS OF THE LAW

NATIVES BELIEVED THAT THIS STAIRWAY WAS CARVED
BY THE ANGELS IN A SINGLE NIGHT

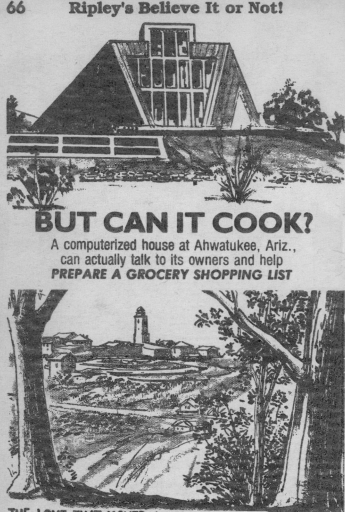

BUT CAN IT COOK?

A computerized house at Ahwatukee, Ariz.,
can actually talk to its owners and help
PREPARE A GROCERY SHOPPING LIST

THE LOVE THAT MOVED AN ENTIRE VILLAGE
CASTELLAR, A COMMUNITY OF 29 HOUSES IN THE
FRENCH ALPS, WAS SHIFTED FROM ONE MOUNTAIN
PEAK TO ANOTHER, IN 1435, AT THE REQUEST
AND EXPENSE OF HENRI LASCARIS -- *SO THE
GIRL HE LOVED WOULD BE NEARER TO HIM*

AN **ASTRONOMICAL OBSERVATORY** FOUND IN THE RUINS OF CHICHEN ITZA, YUCATAN, WAS USED BY MAYA SCIENTISTS IN THE 10th CENT.

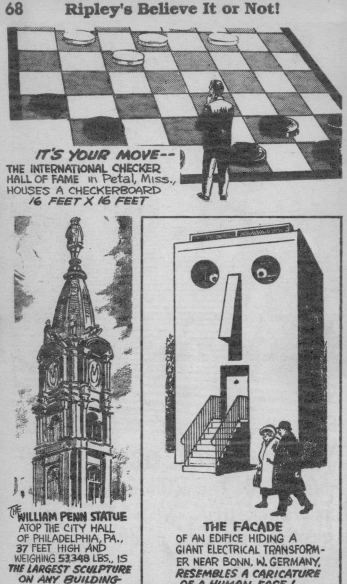

IT'S YOUR MOVE--
THE INTERNATIONAL CHECKER
HALL OF FAME in Petal, Miss.,
HOUSES A CHECKERBOARD
16 FEET X 16 FEET

THE **WILLIAM PENN STATUE**
ATOP THE CITY HALL
OF PHILADELPHIA, PA.,
37 FEET HIGH AND
WEIGHING 53,348 LBS., IS
*THE LARGEST SCULPTURE
ON ANY BUILDING
IN THE WORLD*

THE FACADE
OF AN EDIFICE HIDING A
GIANT ELECTRICAL TRANSFORM-
ER NEAR BONN, W. GERMANY,
*RESEMBLES A CARICATURE
OF A HUMAN FACE !*

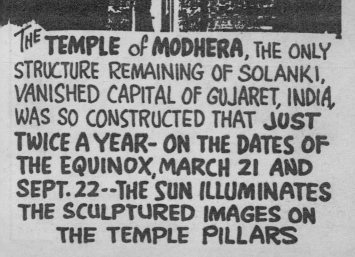

THE **TEMPLE** of **MODHERA**, THE ONLY
STRUCTURE REMAINING OF SOLANKI,
VANISHED CAPITAL OF GUJARET, INDIA,
WAS SO CONSTRUCTED THAT **JUST
TWICE A YEAR-** ON THE DATES OF
THE EQUINOX, MARCH 21 AND
SEPT. 22--THE SUN ILLUMINATES
THE SCULPTURED IMAGES ON
THE TEMPLE PILLARS

THE CEILINGS IN KEENS

a famous New York City restaurant, are
covered with over 50,000 clay pipes that
were smoked by diners after their meal!

STONEHENGE

THE ANCIENT MONUMENT IN WILTSHIRE, ENGLAND,
CONSTRUCTED MORE THAN 3,500 YEARS AGO,
REQUIRED 33 MILLION MAN-HOURS TO BUILD

THE **OXENHAM ARMS**
OF SOUTH ZEAL, ENGLAND,
BUILT AROUND A GRANITE
MONOLITH 800 YEARS AGO,
WAS ORIGINALLY A MONASTERY

THE FRONT DOOR

of the Haskell Free Library and Opera House is in
Derby Line, Vt., in the U.S.A. but its back door
leads to Rock Island in Quebec, Canada, and during
World War II, Canadian patrons who used the front door
HAD TO SHOW THEIR PASSPORTS

AN ANCIENT ROCK CHURCH
LOCATED IN A MOUNTAIN CAVE NEAR LALIBELA,
ETHIOPIA, LOOKS LIKE A BEACHED NOAH'S ARK

LAMU

AN ISLAND OFF THE COAST OF EAST AFRICA HAS A POPULATION OF 31,000 YET NO WHEELED TRAFFIC IS PERMITTED ON THE ISLAND *- NOT EVEN A BICYCLE*

THE MOUNTAIN RESORT THAT IS ALWAYS IN MOTION
GROSSGMEIN, A RESORT VILLAGE IN AUSTRIA, BUILT ON A
ROCKY BASE, IS CONSTANTLY SHIFTING BECAUSE IT RESTS
ON A BED OF SALT 1,000 FEET THICK

THE HOME
OF ROSY AND DAVE
CHILDERS OF
PITTSBURG, KAN.,
IS A 5-STORY,
REMODELED, 60-
YEAR-OLD SILO IN
A CORNFIELD

THE **OLD WINDMILL** of Nantucket, Mass., IS HELD TOGETHER ONLY WITH WOODEN PINS, AND WAS BUILT ENTIRELY FROM TIMBER SALVAGED *FROM WRECKED SHIPS*

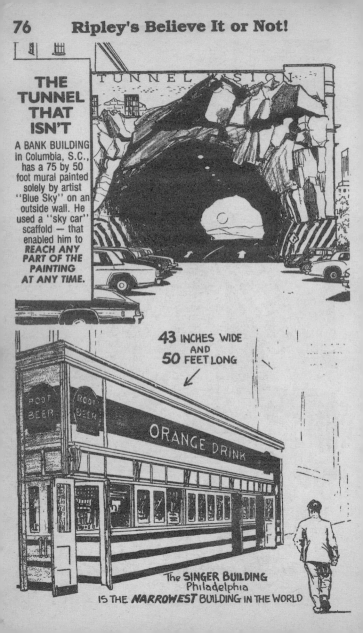

THE TUNNEL THAT ISN'T

A BANK BUILDING in Columbia, S.C., has a 75 by 50 foot mural painted solely by artist ''Blue Sky'' on an outside wall. He used a ''sky car'' scaffold — that enabled him to *REACH ANY PART OF THE PAINTING AT ANY TIME.*

43 INCHES WIDE AND 50 FEET LONG

ROOT BEER

ROOT BEER

ORANGE DRINK

The SINGER BUILDING
Philadelphia
IS THE *NARROWEST* BUILDING IN THE WORLD

THE CAVES OF THE 1,000 BUDDHAS
near Tunhwang, China,
COMPRISE 500 CAVES HOLLOWED
OUT OF A SHEER CLIFF
--AN AREA 10 STORIES HIGH AND A MILE
IN LENGTH, CONSTRUCTED BY BUDDHIST
MONKS OVER A PERIOD OF 1,000 YEARS

THE **WHITE BONES PAGODAS** of LIANGCHOW

THE BONES OF MORE THAN A **MILLION MEN** WHO FELL DURING THE MOHAMMEDAN REBELLION WERE GROUND INTO THE BUILDING MATERIALS TO ERECT THESE TOWERS

Friend and Foe are Mingled in this huge Memorial.

IN RALEIGH, N C, FANS OF STAR TREK ARE ORGANIZING THE ONLY PLANNED COMMUNITY IN THE WORLD WHERE FOLLOWERS CAN *LIVE OUT THE MORAL CODE SET DOWN BY THE POPULAR TELEVISION SHOW!*

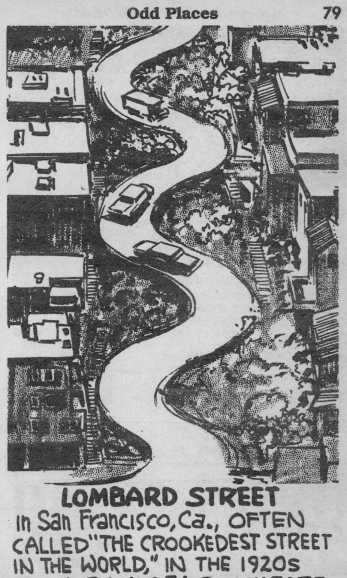

LOMBARD STREET
In San Francisco, Ca., OFTEN CALLED "THE CROOKEDEST STREET IN THE WORLD," IN THE 1920s WAS A **2-WAY THOROUGHFARE**

A MONKEY

that can be clearly seen only from the air in the
desert region of Nacza, Peru, and measuring 260 feet
from head to tail, is one of about 30 baffling huge drawings
*MADE BY ANCIENT PERUVIANS BETWEEN
1000 B.C. AND 1000 A.D.*

THE WORKMEN

removing a window on a balcony of Irmgard Freisleben's
home in Frankfurt, West Germany, actually is a
REALISTIC MURAL PAINTED AROUND THE WINDOW!

THE STRANGEST "TORNADOES" IN ALL NATURE
HUGE COLUMNS OF SAND APPEAR SUDDENLY
IN THE SONORA DESERT, IN MEXICO,
AND MYSTERIOUSLY WHIRL VIOLENTLY
-- ALTHOUGH THERE IS NOT THE
SLIGHTEST BREEZE IN THE AREA

The **INTERNATIONAL PEACE HOSPITAL** in Northwestern China, CONSISTS OF INDIVIDUAL CAVES *BUILT INTO A MOUNTAIN*

The **NOISIEST APARTMENT HOUSE** AN APARTMENT HOUSE IN ZURICH, SWITZERLAND, WAS BUILT WITH A TUNNEL THROUGH ITS SECOND FLOOR FOR AN ELEVATED STREET CAR LINE

JACOB'S LADDER
on St. Helena's Island,
a concrete stairway
built in 1932, is
933 FEET LONG!

the **TEMPLE THAT HAS BEEN REBUILT 64 TIMES!**
THE SHRINE OF NAIKU at Ise, Japan, FIRST CONSTRUCTED IN THE YEAR 685, HAS BEEN DEMOLISHED AND THEN RESTORED *EVERY 20 YEARS*

SAN FRANCISCO, CA. HAS 92.6 RESTAURANTS PER SQ. MILE -- MORE THAN ANY OTHER CITY IN THE U.S.-- ONE FOR EVERY 164 RESIDENTS AND COULD SEAT THE CITY'S ENTIRE POPULATION OF 705,000 *SIMULTANEOUSLY*

The ALL-GLASS CHURCH
Tubize, Belgium
THE ENTIRE STRUCTURE CONSISTS OF GLASS ERECTED UPON A GLASS FOUNDATION

A SINGLE TREE
STANDS IN THE CENTER OF THE TENERE WASTE
-- A 600-MILE AREA OF THE SAHARA --
YET, ONCE THE ENTIRE COUNTRY WAS
COVERED WITH LUXURIANT VEGETATION

THE RANI KA NAUR
IN THE UDAYAGIRI HILL   IN ORISSA, INDIA,
IS THE LARGEST PALACE IN THE WORLD
LOCATED ENTIRELY INSIDE A CAVE

THE TEMPLE OF ALL FAITHS
BIRLA TEMPLE
in New Delhi, India, INCLUDES
SEPARATE AREAS FOR WORSHIP
FOR EVERY KNOWN RELIGION

THE OLYMPIC STADIUM in Helsinki, Finland,
IS A HUGE SUNDIAL
SPORT FANS CAN ALWAYS TELL THE TIME
BY THE SHADOW OF THE STADIUM TOWER

CUMBERLAND FALLS in Kentucky, 150 FEET WIDE
AND 68 FEET HIGH, *FORMS A MOONBOW
EACH TIME THERE IS A FULL MOON*
THE ONLY OTHER WATERFALL IN THE WORLD THAT
DISPLAYS A MOONBOW IS AFRICA'S VICTORIA FALLS

A **CHAPEL** FOR VISITORS
TO REAL DE CATORCE, MEXICO
--CARVED IN THE WALLS OF
THE OLD MINING TUNNEL
THAT LEADS INTO THE TOWN

THE **WHIRLING CLOUD** of MOUNT JIRINAJ (Indonesia)

A FLAT CLOUD
HOVERING OVER THE PEAK OF AN EXTINCT VOLCANO
AFFECTED BY HOT AIR RISING FROM THE CRATER,
SPINS SWIFTLY AROUND AND AROUND

THE LEANING "TOWER" OF JAPAN
A HOUSE IN SHIZUOKA CITY, WHICH SEEMS TO HAVE
BEEN GOBBLED UP BY THE EARTH, WAS DESIGNED
SPECIFICALLY TO ALERT RESIDENTS TO A
PREDICTED EARTHQUAKE

DEDE

A VILLAGE IN THE BED OF
THE YANGTZE RIVER, CHINA,
IS INHABITED FOR ONLY 3 WINTER
MONTHS *BECAUSE IT IS UNDER
WATER THE OTHER 9
MONTHS OF EACH YEAR*

THE CHURCH of **CHRIST** in BASSENDEAN, AUSTRALIA,
WAS CONSTRUCTED IN A SINGLE DAY
IT WAS BUILT BY **120** VOLUNTEERS ON JAN. 4, 1913,
AND SERVICES WERE HELD IN IT THE NEXT DAY

INFLATION in the 12TH CENTURY
THE **CHATEAU** de **VOUFFLENS** in Switzerland,
WAS EXCHANGED BY GUILLELME de WOLFLENS
FOR A NEW COAT FOR HIS WIFE   (1175)

THE WORLD'S LARGEST COFFEEPOT

A GIANT COFFEEPOT LOCATED ATOP A TOWER IN STANTON, IOWA, IS 36 FT. HIGH, 20 FT. WIDE, 6 FT. DEEP AND COULD HOLD 640,000 CUPS OF COFFEE

THE HOOBER STAND near Rawmarsh, England, WAS BUILT HIGH ENOUGH TO OVERLOOK EXACTLY 50 CHURCHES AND 50 COAL MINES

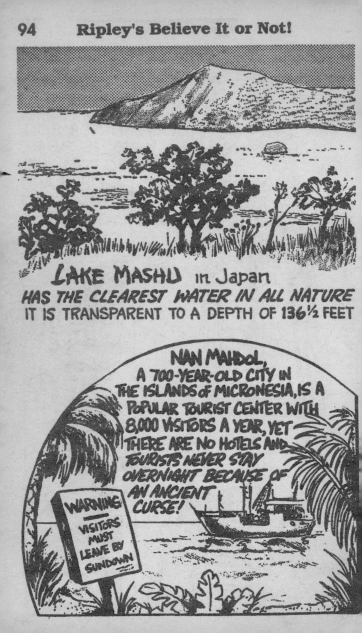

LAKE MASHU in Japan
HAS THE CLEAREST WATER IN ALL NATURE
IT IS TRANSPARENT TO A DEPTH OF 136½ FEET

NAN MADOL, A 700-YEAR-OLD CITY IN THE ISLANDS OF MICRONESIA, IS A POPULAR TOURIST CENTER WITH 8,000 VISITORS A YEAR, YET THERE ARE NO HOTELS AND TOURISTS NEVER STAY OVERNIGHT BECAUSE OF AN ANCIENT CURSE!

WARNING
—
VISITORS MUST LEAVE BY SUNDOWN

THE **LEANING TOWER OF PISA** WAS BEGUN IN THE 12th CENTURY AND NOT COMPLETED UNTIL THE 14th-- BUT ITS LEANING WAS APPARENT AFTER ONLY THREE OF ITS EIGHT STORIES HAD BEEN BUILT

PUSHKAR near Ajmere, India,
IS CONSIDERED SO SACRED THAT
WITHIN THE TOWN LIMITS
IT IS A SIN TO KILL A FLY

"**NOTHING**"
A TOWN IN THE ARID DESERT
OF N.W. ARIZONA, CONSISTS OF
A SNACK BAR, A GARAGE
AND A POPULATION OF
ONLY 4 PEOPLE

NOTHING

THAT'S NOTHING!

THE SEEING EYE TEMPLE!
of Kathmandu, Nepal

THE UBIQUITOUS EYES PAINTED UPON THE TEMPLE
LOOK STRAIGHT INTO THE HEART OF A SINNER —
AND ARE THE GREATEST DETERRENT to CRIME IN THE CITY!

THE HOMES

OF THE 30,000 RESIDENTS OF THE BOROUGH OF SANTIAGO
IN GUADIX, SPAIN, ARE ALL CAVES CARVED IN THE MOUNTAIN
–EACH EQUIPPED WITH ELECTRIC LIGHT AND TILED FLOORS
AND SELLING FOR $35 TO $350 EACH
THE ROCK IS SO SOFT IT CAN BE CUT LIKE CHEESE, AND
THE CAVES ARE WARM IN WINTER AND COOL IN SUMMER

HOUSE IN 2 COUNTRIES

THE HOME OF THE LATE JOHN MOORE
NEAR SWEETGRASS, MONTANA,
*HAS ITS BEDROOM IN THE UNITED STATES
AND ITS KITCHEN IN CANADA*

THE SMALLEST HOUSE IN ENGLAND
A HOME ON CONWAY QUAI, NORTH
WALES, 72 INCHES WIDE, 100
INCHES DEEP AND 122 IN. HIGH

KANAKANAK
KAYAK
KAMAK
KANAK
KIJIK
KAK

TOWNS AND ISLANDS
IN ALASKA
-- *WHICH READ THE SAME*
FORWARD OR BACKWARD

YELLOW PINE, IDAHO
DEEP IN THE MOUNTAINOUS BOISE
NATIONAL FOREST, IS 52 MILES
FROM THE CLOSEST TOWN AND CAN
BE REACHED ONLY BY SKIPLANE
DURING WINTER — YET ITS
RESIDENTS SO VALUE THEIR
ISOLATION AND INDEPENDENCE
*THAT THEY REFUSE TO HAVE
A SINGLE TELEPHONE!*

THE **FLATTEST FLAT** IN THE WORLD

AN ARCHITECTURAL
ECCENTRICITY IN ALEXANDRIA, EGYPT.
A FAMILY OF 5 LIVES IN 3 ROOMS HUNG ON A WALL

A **DWELLING** in Airth, Stirlingshire, England, BUILT AS A SUMMER HOUSE IN 1761, IS SHAPED LIKE A *PINEAPPLE*

THE TRAVELING SCHOOLHOUSES
SEVERAL PUBLIC SCHOOLS in Northern Ontario, ARE RAILROAD CARS WHICH SPEND 5 DAYS EVERY 5 WEEKS IN EACH AREA

HOOVER DAM

ON THE COLORADO RIVER BETWEEN ARIZONA AND NEVADA, IS 726 FT. TALL, THE HEIGHT OF A 60-STORY SKYSCRAPER, AND WEIGHS MORE THAN 6,500,000 TONS ... THE 3,250,000 CU. YARDS OF CONCRETE USED IN ITS CONSTRUCTION ARE ENOUGH TO PAVE A HIGHWAY FROM NEW YORK TO CALIFORNIA

AN OFFICE BUILDING

in Turlock, Calif., was designed to look like a
GIANT BULLDOZER!

LAKE EYRE

AUSTRALIA'S LARGEST DRY LAKE,
COVERING AN AREA OF 5,000 SQ.
MILES, *HAS HELD WATER
ONLY TWICE IN HISTORY*

THE TOWN of DUIRAT
in Southern Tunisia
IS ENTIRELY LOCATED
INSIDE A SINGLE MOUNTAIN

THE **TOWN ON WHEELS**
*LAKEWOOD, in Western Australia,
A COMMUNITY IN THE HEART OF THE LUMBER AND GOLD MINING AREA
HAS ITS HOMES, SHOPS, POST OFFICE AND POLICE STATION
MOUNTED ON RAILROAD CARS*

RESTAURANT DINERS in Zahle,
a resort town in Lebanon,
*SIT AT TABLES THAT STRADDLE
BRANCHES OF THE BARDUNI RIVER*

THE WHITE RIVER
MONSTER SANCTUARY
IN NEWPORT, ARK.,
WAS CREATED BY THE
STATE'S LEGISLATURE WHICH
MADE IT ILLEGAL TO "MOLEST,
KILL OR TRAMPLE" ON A
LEGENDARY SEA MONSTER

THE GROVE PARK INN

in Asheville, N.C., built in 1913 has two huge fireplaces
in its lobby each some 34 feet wide and over 19 feet high
— *WITH ELEVATORS LOCATED INSIDE THEIR ROCKWORK*

THE SKY BATHERS
A HOTEL ON HONSHU, JAPAN'S WAKAYAMA PENINSULA,
OFFERS HOT-SPRING BATHS IN A CABLE CAR
AS IT TRAVERSES A DEEP GORGE

ᵀᴴᴱ**AMAZING BARN OF LEIXLIP**
Ireland
IT IS 73 FEET HIGH, WITH AN
OUTSIDE CIRCULAR STAIRWAY
OF 94 STEPS, AND WAS BUILT
DURING THE FAMINE OF 1742
*TO PROVIDE EMPLOYMENT
FOR THE NEEDY*

A SIX-STORY PYRAMID

THE HOME OF WAUKEGAN, ILL., CONTRACTOR JIM ONAN AND FAMILY, IS COVERED WITH 24-KARAT GOLD PLATE, SURROUNDED BY A MOAT, HAS 17,000 SQ.FT. OF SPACE AND IS BUILT AT *ONE-NINTH THE SCALE OF EGYPT'S GREAT PYRAMID!*

A CITY GATE
In Ayassoluk, Turkey,
BUILT BY THE GREEKS 1,600
YEARS AGO, WAS CONSTRUCTED
*OUT OF TOMBSTONES
AND COFFIN LIDS*

HOUSES IN THE MARKET PLACE OF KITZINGEN, GERMANY, WERE CONSTRUCTED OF MORTAR MIXED WITH WINE -- *THE FRAGRANCE OF WHICH IS NOTICEABLE THROUGHOUT THE AREA*

THE **WELL** OF **DOON** Donegal, Ireland,

IS SURROUNDED WITH BANDAGES AND CRUTCHES, ABANDONED BY VISITORS CONVINCED THAT THEY WERE CURED *MERELY BY DRINKING ITS WATERS*

THE ARMOUR-STINER HOUSE IN IRVINGTON ON THE HUDSON, N·Y· WAS BUILT IN 1860 TO REPRESENT *A HUMAN BRAIN*

ITS ROOMS WERE LAID OUT ACCORDING TO THE PRINCIPLES OF PHRENOLOGY, THE PSEUDOSCIENCE WHICH MAINTAINED THAT BUMPS ON THE HEAD HAVE AN EFFECT ON PERSONALITY

THE CHAPEL OF REMONOT
France
EXCEPT FOR ITS BELFRY
IS COMPLETELY UNDERGROUND
IT WAS CARVED OUT OF
SOLID ROCK IN ANCIENT
TIMES AS A PROTECTION
AGAINST PAGAN ATTACKS

**THE FIRST CALENDAR WAS
THE GREAT PYRAMID OF CHEOPS!**
THE SHADOW CAST BY THE PYRAMID ENABLED THE EGYPTIANS
TO DISCOVER THE RELATIONSHIP OF THE EARTH AND THE SUN,
THE 4 SEASONS, AND OUR MODERN METHOD OF MEASURING TIME—
THE FIRST YEAR DETERMINED BY THIS CALENDAR WAS 4236 B.C.

THE **FROZEN WATERFALL** of Mt. Beardmore, in the Antarctic
HAS A HEIGHT OF MORE THAN 10,000 FEET
— 60 TIMES THAT OF NIAGARA FALLS

A HUGE WALL

THAT STOOD FOR YEARS
BESIDE A RAILROAD
STATION IN SASKATCHEWAN, CAN.,
*WAS CONSTRUCTED OF
THE SKULLS AND BONES
OF MORE THAN
25,000 BUFFALO*

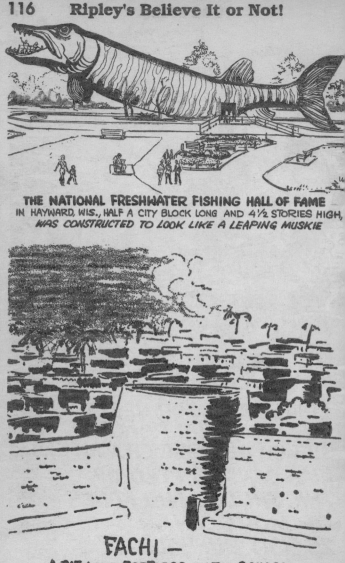

THE NATIONAL FRESHWATER FISHING HALL OF FAME
IN HAYWARD, WIS., HALF A CITY BLOCK LONG AND 4½ STORIES HIGH,
WAS CONSTRUCTED TO LOOK LIKE A LEAPING MUSKIE

FACHI —
A CITY AND FORTRESS IN THE SAHARA
BUILT ENTIRELY OF SALT.

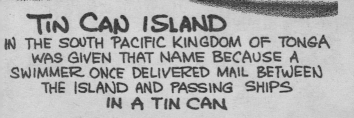

TIN CAN ISLAND
IN THE SOUTH PACIFIC KINGDOM OF TONGA
WAS GIVEN THAT NAME BECAUSE A
SWIMMER ONCE DELIVERED MAIL BETWEEN
THE ISLAND AND PASSING SHIPS
IN A TIN CAN

THE UPSIDE-DOWN HOTEL
THE HOTEL du LAC in TUNIS, TUNISIA, LOOKS LIKE AN UPSIDE DOWN STAIRCASE

CARHENGE

JAMES REINDERS of ALLIANCE, NE, BUILT A MONUMENT USING DOZENS OF HALF-BURIED OLD CARS SET IN A PATTERN *THAT RESEMBLES ENGLAND'S STONEHENGE!*

EVERY BUILDING
in Ochiltree, Texas
WHEN THE RAILROAD BYPASSED IT IN THE 1920s,
WAS HITCHED TO HUGE TRACTORS AND MOVED
TO A NEW SITE ALONG THE RAILROAD

THE WORLD'S DEEPEST LAKE
LAKE BAYKAL
IN THE SIBERIAN REGION OF THE U.S.S.R.
IS 5,315 FEET DEEP

THE WORLD'S STRANGEST NATIVITY SCENE
COMPLETE WITH REPLICAS OF THE HOLY CHILD, MARY,
JOSEPH AND STABLE ANIMALS, IS PRESENTED ANNUALLY
IN AMALFI, ITALY, AT THE BASE OF THE GROTTA SMERALDA
--THIRTY FEET BELOW THE SURFACE OF THE MEDITER-
RANEAN SEA, *WHERE IT CAN BE REACHED
ONLY BY DIVERS*

SURTSEY AN ISLAND NAMED FOR NORSE MYTHOLOGY'S FIRE GIANT, SURTUR, WAS BORN ON NOV. 14, 1963, WHEN AN UNDERSEA VOLCANO ERUPTED IN THE NORTH ATLANTIC NEAR ICELAND. TWO MONTHS LATER, AFTER CONTINUOUS ERUPTIONS, IT HAD RISEN TO A HEIGHT OF 670 FEET. NOW PEOPLED WITH FLORA AND FAUNA, IT IS EXPECTED TO LAST A THOUSAND YEARS

THE **BED** OF THE KURUK-DARYA RIVER IN CENTRAL ASIA *WAS BONE DRY FOR 1,600 YEARS—* ITS WATERS RETURNED IN 1934 AND THE RIVER HAS FLOWED NORMALLY EVER SINCE

THE HOUSE THAT'S NOT A HOUSE!
23 LEINSTER GARDENS IN THE BAYSWATER SECTION OF LONDON, ENGLAND, WHICH APPEARS TO BE A HANDSOME 4-STORY APARTMENT BUILDING, *ACTUALLY IS A DUMMY FAÇADE PAINTED ON A CEMENT WALL TO CONCEAL THE ENTRANCE TO A SUBWAY TUNNEL*

THE TEMPLE OF MATS
ON SACRED ISLAND, JAPAN,
IS DECORATED WITH
HUNDREDS OF WOODEN
RICE SPOONS

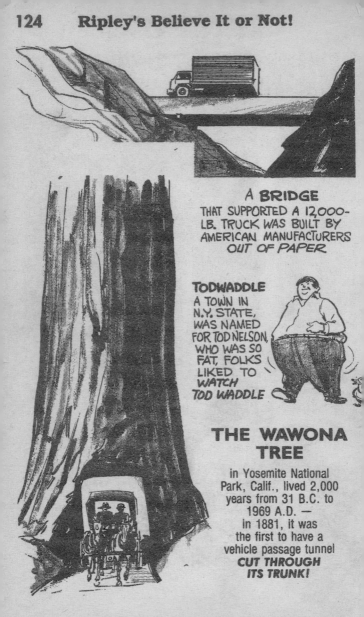

A **BRIDGE**
THAT SUPPORTED A 12,000-LB. TRUCK WAS BUILT BY AMERICAN MANUFACTURERS *OUT OF PAPER*

TODWADDLE
A TOWN IN N.Y. STATE, WAS NAMED FOR TOD NELSON, WHO WAS SO FAT, FOLKS LIKED TO *WATCH TOD WADDLE*

THE WAWONA TREE
in Yosemite National Park, Calif., lived 2,000 years from 31 B.C. to 1969 A.D. — in 1881, it was the first to have a vehicle passage tunnel *CUT THROUGH ITS TRUNK!*